D1179888

Palette Of COURAGE

MARNEY PIKE

AN ARTIST'S JOURNEY TO UNDERSTANDING

© 2005 by Woodford Press
All rights reserved under the Pan-American and International Copyright Conventions

Printed in China

This book may not be reproduced in whole or in part, in any form or by any means, electronic or mechanical, including photocopying, recording, or by any information storage and retrieval system now known or hereafter invented, without written permission from the publisher.

ISBN 0-9767743-0-5

Design by Richard Ferguson
Cover art *Courage* by Marney Pike

To Order visit:

www.marneysart.com

Or call:

503•450•0878

e-mail: *marney@marnysart.com*

Woodford Press Book Publishers
1025 S.W. Myrtle Dr.
Portland, OR 97201
503•450•0878

Contents

INTRODUCTION

I was in my fifties and, like so many others, saw life rushing by. At times, it seemed like a torrent, racing past in a way that I felt I was an observer more than an active participant. My children were grown, my husband was busy with his work and many interests and there I was— wondering where to focus my own life. I was ready for the next chapter. The only question, of course, was, what was that chapter going to be?

Unlike my previous obligations of raising three children and being available for whatever their needs were, volunteering in my community and helping my husband build his career, it was clear to me this next pursuit was one I had to define for myself. I could not just let it "happen." It was with a combination of trepidation and anticipation, that I reached out and took the challenge. I actively wrote the next chapter of my life. It's true— part of the chapter had bumps. It was those bumps, however, that helped me find my deep passion and precious gift for painting. With that discovery, my life was transformed. My passion became my purpose.

Palette of Courage was written to inspire others searching for their own passion and for their own purpose. As you read this small book filled with my personal experiences and feelings, I hope you will think about your own palette of courage and where it can take you. I wish you a wonderful journey.

Nancy Pike

Self Portrait
Acrylic on Paper
13"x 9.25"

My Life, My Paintings

I look at my life as a party with many guests arriving.

Some are dear close friends.

Some from far away places, all playing a role in my life. I welcome some with tenderness. Yet others frighten me. Others bring up emotions of hostility, curiosity, control, and playfulness. My paintings are a cross-section of those guests.

I would like to introduce you to them,

one

at

a

time.

Nancy Pike

Restlessness

I think creative people, in general, are restless.

It is a feeling of wanting to jump from one thing to the next. It is getting bored very easily. It is like little *butterflies* jumping all over you, running around. Sometimes you reject restraints. It's a little like a bird, *flying*.

You want to just soar. You don't want any barriers around you.

When you get that feeling of restlessness you are neither here nor there.

Limbo. Stuck in between. You don't know where the next step is going or where the next energy is going to come from.

Some of my favorite paintings were *born* when I was most restless.

In A Circular Path
Acrylic on Paper
17"x 25.5"

Feelings

You can feel too deeply and sometimes you don't know how to get rid of the feeling. You carry it with you. If someone hurts, you take it on yourself. You hurt for them. You have their pain. What a load to carry. At times, it's too big a load. Sometimes feeling is a *curse*.

But, I am learning to embrace rather than fear the *darkness*. I know that even in *darkness*, there is color. It is not just plain *black*.

Feelings
Acrylic on Paper
15"x 22.5"

SEQUINED BASEBALL HATS

It happened in my fifties

The sequins on my blouses

The **silver** and **gold** high heels

And **black** stockings

Red-sequined
belting around my waist

Breaking out of the mold

Courage to expose myself

Then tucked away in a box

Part of my evolving tapestry

Sequined Baseball Hats
Acrylic on Canvas
12.5"x 9"

Growing

Sometimes I've had to grow into a painting. Maybe it took me further than I knew I could go. I may have been in a subconscious state and wasn't even *aware* of where I was.

So it's good to just step back and *stretch* as you look into it. Observe it, live with it. Massage it in your *heart and in your eyes*

I would say the majority of my paintings have gone further than I thought I could go, personally and as an artist.

Breakers
Acrylic on Paper
13"x 16"

The Approach
Acrylic on Canvas
33.75"x 35"

Fear

Fear *holds me paralyzed and stops me from going forward.*

It deprives me of growth, holds me as a prisoner within myself

I can't just sit on my bed and cry

I have to take charge; it's my life

I ask myself, "What would be the most terrible thing if I **fail***?"*

Would I die?

When I confront and conquer my fears through painting, I **feel** *empowered.*

h a p p i n e

Still Life
Acrylic on Canvas
30"x56"

S S

When you are there, happiness is wonderful. It's like finishing a painting and saying,

"Wow! Look what I did!"

It's elation that is grandiose But it comes when it wants to come. You can't always expect it.

For me to experience happiness, I had to know what was inside of me. What could I bring out? Was there anything there to bring out? A part of me felt dead. There was no life inside. For happiness to arrive inside of me, I needed to feel passionate about something.

Painting, for me, is joy. It is purpose.

Courage
Acrylic on Canvas
22"x 28"

COURAGE

Sometimes just stepping out of **bed**, putting your **shoes** on, or brushing your **teeth** takes courage. Sometimes you have to tackle what seem like thorns.

Then those **thorns** can become your friend instead of foe. You are no longer ***afraid*** of them.

For me, ***c o u r a g e*** is always looking, learning, stretching, tackling unknowns. It meant getting in touch with my dark side, embracing it rather than running from it

Plowing through the secret crevices inside myself is my courage.

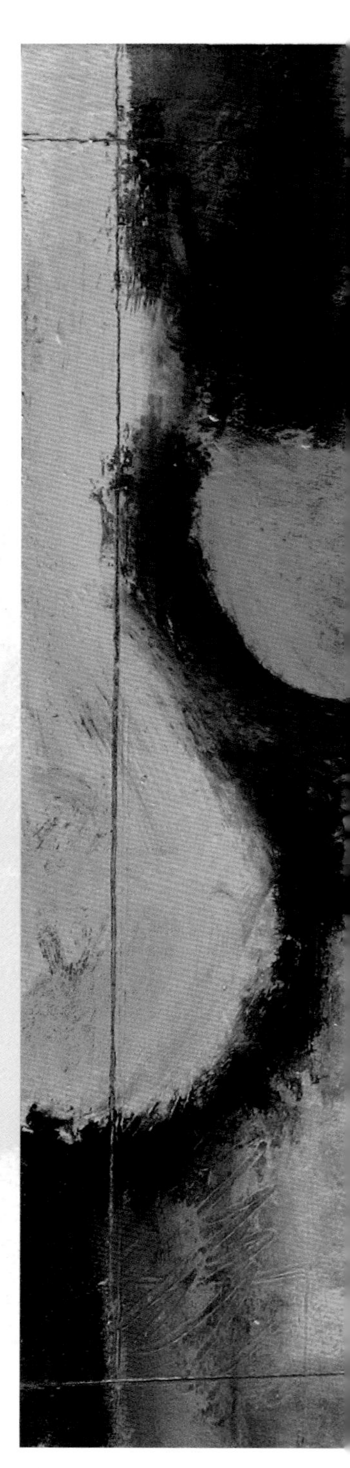

cour•age

Sometimes we're not even aware that the call is out

Every ounce of energy is summoned

From down deep in your psyche, courage emerges

Forcing itself forward

I act

Feeling proud as a peacock with feathers spread

Time for courage to rest until it's summoned again

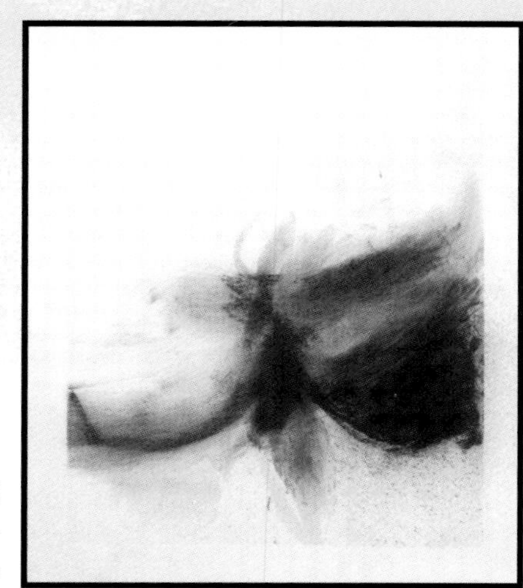

Detail
Ink On Paper
13.5"x 11"

Courageous
Acrylic on Canvas
22"x 28"

TURMOIL

Sometimes it's easier to say what I don't feel

There is no calm
There is no tranquility
There is no peace from within

The turmoil is like a stormy ocean deep in my gut
The waves want to crash thru my ribs

I feel unsettled, insecure and threatened

On the outside, I present a façade to the public

What I want them to see
What they want to see

SEE
SEE
SEE

AND

I struggle to understand it
I struggle to resolve the conflict
I struggle to make peace with it

I struggle for the turmoil to end.....When it leaves.....I'll be whole again.....

A NEW CHAPTER BEGINS

Turmoil
Acrylic on Canvas
16"x 20"

Passage
Acrylic on Canvas
12.5"x 9"

Taking A Chance
Acrylic on Canvas
20"x 16"

Finding Home

The best part of painting is when I become totally immersed.

It's like I am in a meditative state with nothing around.

I'm totally focused.

It's like being enveloped in the embrace of a pool of warm water.

Not caring about anything else.

Just carrying myself to where everything is and should be.

It is the most peaceful place in the world.

My own space.

I'm home.

Ink on Paper
14"x16.5"

Traveler
Acrylic on Paper
27.75"x 20"

eXperimenting

My studio is a laboratory. It's a room full of "what ifs?" What if I took some black paint and watered it down and put a little burnt umber in there?

What if I covered the whole

painting and let it dry for a few minutes and then

burnt umber washed it off?

What if I did that? What would happen?

I may find something wonderful.

I must begin. If I don't take the risk, how will I know?

burnt umber

Pushing It
Multimedia
20"x16"

Passion Ignited

Finding out what was stirring inside me was not always fun.

I learned a great deal about myself. My fabric . My landscape. I tried all sorts of possibilities.

When I finally and by accident landed on painting, it turned me into a different person. I dreamt in color. I could see my paintings in my dreams. The days went by quickly and I never got tired. I couldn't wait to get to my paintings and make my magic.

My mind seemed to be a sponge, learning the language of painting. It was an exquisite challenge.

It was also a journey of hard work.

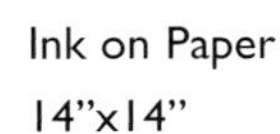

Ink on Paper
14"x14"

Passion Ignited
Acrylic on Canvas
21"x 28"

PLAYING CARDS

Life deals our daily hand

We try to make sense of it

The next day

Another deal

And another

Each person's hand is unique

Always different, always challenging

Playing out the hand gives me purpose

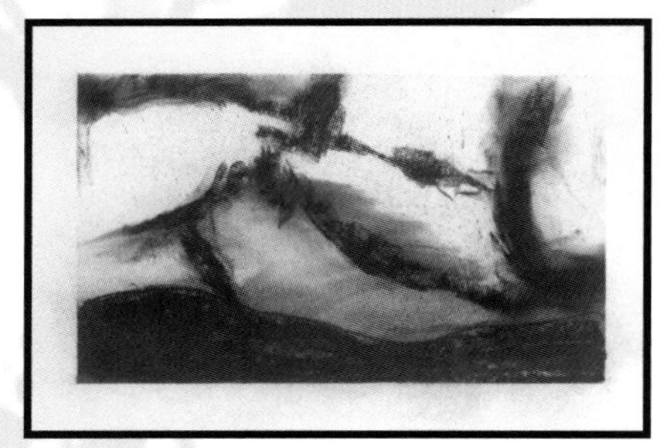

Ink on Paper
10"x16.5"

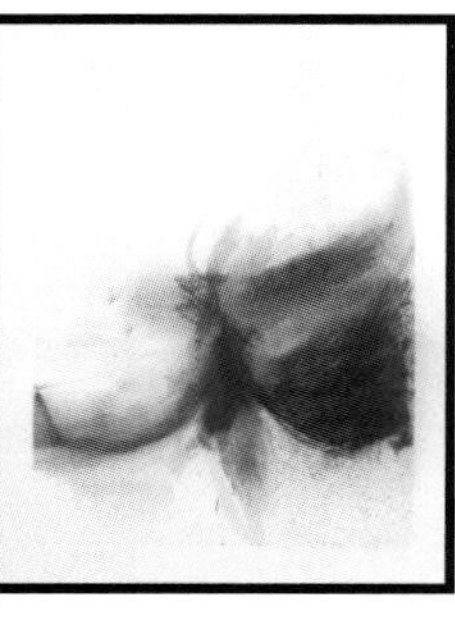

Ink on Paper
13.5"x11"

Texas Hold'em
Acrylic on Wood
9"x 8"

The Journey

Traveling the day can be adventurous, joyous or sad

My mind sifts through all these feelings

I must make sense of them

but

No lingering

Let's go on

i must

I have places to go,

People to ***see***

Things to do

Stopping is not an option

What places lay ahead?

Mah Jongg
Acrylic on Wood
9"x 8"

rest

At times

I need to rest from growing

Energy subsides

Time to regroup

Time to gather —
for my sights —
for my smells —
for my touches —

My battery re-energizes

Ink on Paper
13.5"x 10.5"

Acrylic on Paper
28"x 20.5"

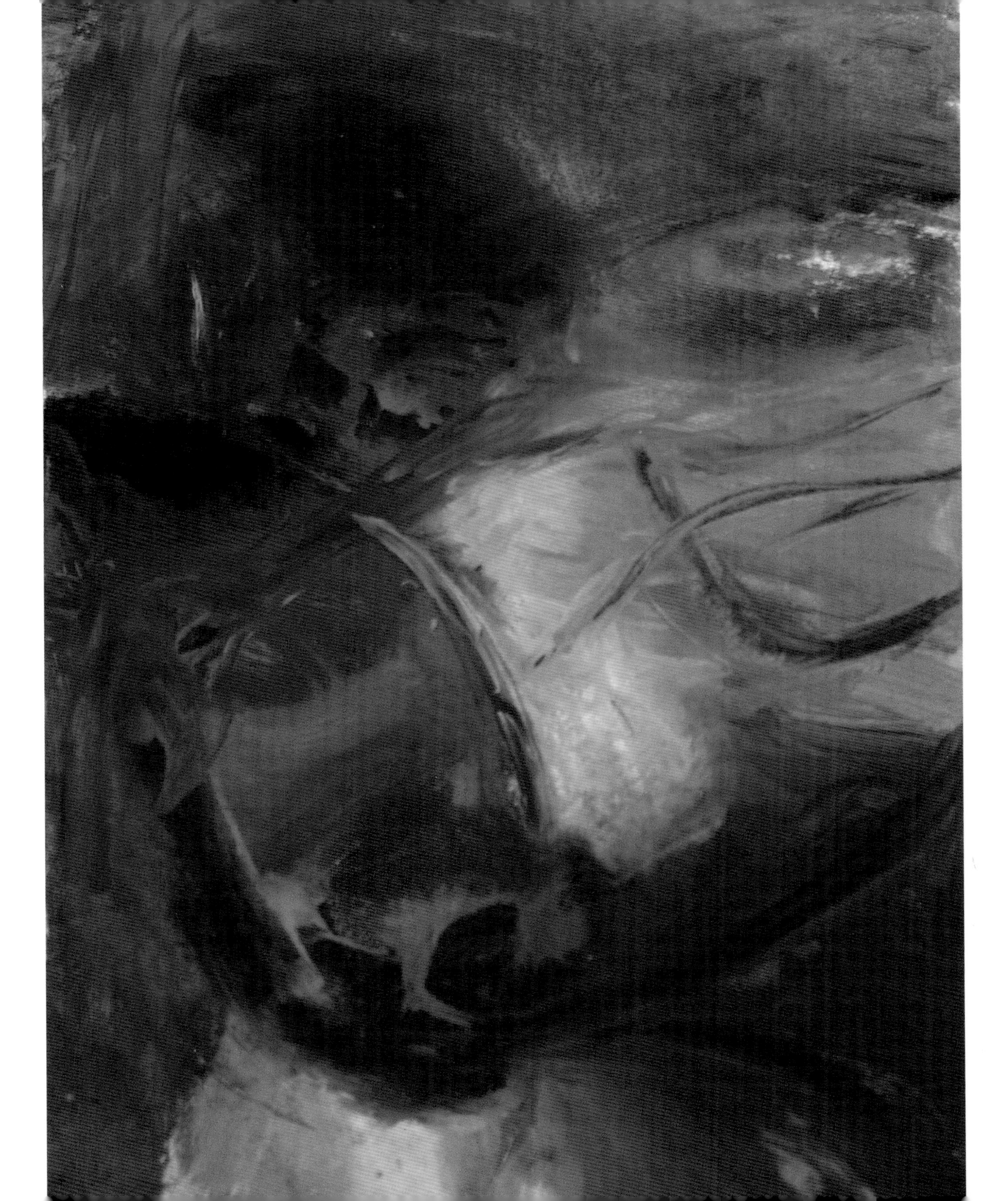

Walking

Up at 6 AM
Time to Think
Shaking loose the cobwebs
Facing all that holds me back

Walking

Seeing the beauty of nature
The ups and downs of the sidewalk
Feeling the warmth of friendships
Old and New
How far I have come
What Next?
I'm refreshed

Ink on Paper
13.5"x 10.5"

Acrylic on Canvas
12..5"x9"

Walking At 6 AM
Acrylic on Paper
11.5"x 8.25"

Time To Think
Acrylic on Paper
11.5"x 8.25"

Refreshed
Acrylic on Paper
11.5"x 8.25"

Getting

Emerging
Acrylic on Wood
8"x 9"

Started

Being creative is not a 9-5 job. At times you feel paralyzed. Nothing happens. Thoughts stop. Your imagination gone. You are looking at a **blank canvas** *and it stays that way for a long time. You make every excuse imaginable.*

The muse is not always there. It's taking a long lunch. Went on a trip somewhere and hasn't yet returned.

Ink on Paper
13.5"x 10.5"

I ask myself

"How can I be so passionate about something that is so difficult and unpredictable. Is painting my friend or foe?"

Ink on Paper
13.5"x 10.5"

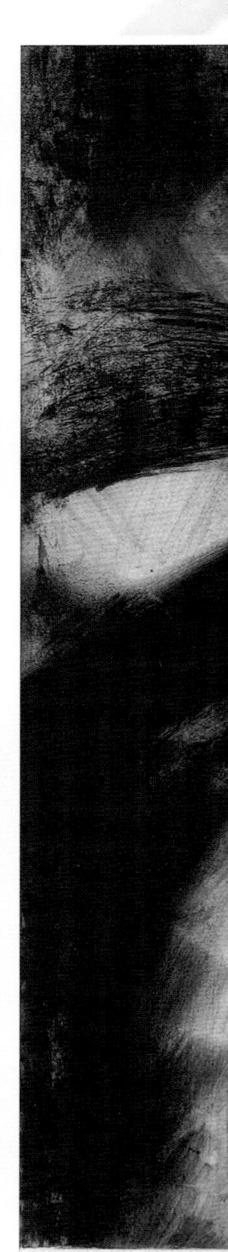

Three Nudes
Acrylic on Paper
20.5"x28"

Free Spirit

Music and rhythm set me free

Often while painting I listen to music

Sometimes I don't even know what color I have in hand.

It doesn't matter

I hold the brush and feel myself moving to the rhythm

It's not just brush strokes

My whole body is moving. But

the euphoria is short-lived. It comes and goes quickly.

During that brief moment

I know that I'm a free spirit

The Search
Acrylic on Paper
20"x34"

The Search

I was always searching for one
piece — that missing piece.

Passion.
Something I could call my own.

I loved my family, my children
and husband.

But everyone was moving on
and I needed to do the same.

The next chapter was mine. But
where to begin?

Today, I introduce myself as a
painter.

Inner Self
Acrylic on Wood
9"x 8"

Nurturing the Self

We know how to care for our exterior.
We know how to get a massage, a
facial, Get some new clothes, new ear-
rings, even mascara.

What we don't know how to do is
take care of our interior self.

Our Soul.

The Heart.

The part that Beats.

Taking care of yourself takes courage.
You have to say "no"
in order to do what you want.

Sometimes it's rearranging obligations.
Sometimes it's taking a break from
friends

You don't need permission to nurture
yourself.

It's Okay.

Ink on Paper
13.5"x 10.5"

Personal Space

A place where I feel protected

And surrounded by comfort

Where I surrender myself to

M o o d s

C r e a t i v i t y

Where tubes of paints are separated by color

Brushes worn and tattered in old jars

Some waiting for their experience with paint

That special place called

My Room* • • • *My Space* • • • *My Studio

Caught Between
Acrylic on Wood
9"x 8"

Impatience

Distractions
Focusing
Always getting up
Taking a walk
A cup of tea sounds good
Making a phone call
Playing with my puppy
Let's see
Natures calling
Need a little nourishing
Back at table
Can I write now••• Yes•••No
Who knows?
Another 20 minutes pass
Talk to myself "Lets get something done"
A friend calls – We talk
What's wrong with me?
Something pulls me back
Low and behold I've finished
Yes, I've done my project
It's great
Feeling good once again
Sigh of relief

tea
•••Yes
•••No

Blue
Acrylic on Wood
9"x 8"

Community

A delicious pie sliced in sections

Some labeled family, friends, colleagues, and more

I share thoughts and ideas with some

Intimate feelings with others

They celebrate with me

And I, them

A delicious pie sliced in sections
Some labeled family, friends, colleagues, and more
I share thoughts and ideas with some
Intimate feelings with others
They celebrate with me
And I, them

Support
Acrylic on Wood
9"x 8"

Beauty

Engages and soothes my soul
It's the view from the house
The glow of the mountains
The setting sun saying good-night
The dreams that come true

And
those
yet
to
come

Scenic Dream
Acrylic on Wood
9"x 8"

Love

Love has many faces
It is a smile that happens inside of you
A feeling of
contentment

Love caresses and embraces *you*
In a soft, tender way

Some loves are deeper than others
Hurt more than others
Make you smile more than others
But the most important love is loving yourself

NOW

Embrace
Acrylic on Paper
28"x 20.5"

Marney and Rosie

The Author and The Artist

Marney grew up with three brothers in Worcester, Massachusetts and has lived in Portland, Oregon since 1965. She and her husband of 41 years have raised three children, Michelle, Steven, and Jamie.

Marney has always been involved in numerous community activities, including working on PTA projects, the Portland Jewish Federation Women's Board, and the Portland Museum Contemporary Art Council Board. Always artistic and creative, she began a serious pursuit of painting in 1995, when she was mentored by prominent Portland artist Ted Katz. Her art has been shown in respected galleries. Additionally, Marney enjoys speaking to groups about her transition from full time motherhood to achieving her full potential.